CW00411185

micro:bit basics

A first guide for hobbyists, students and teachers of the BBC's 'microbit' programmable computer.

www.microbitbasics.com

Contents

About the Book

For some time now I've been looking for a suitable subject to provide the basis of a new book project. Specifically, I've been looking to write about a potentially disruptive technology that is cheap (so that virtually anyone can use it), supported by a "big name" organization (to assure wide take-up of the technology), and which is aligned with my experience as a technical author and former computer programmer. I have found the perfect subject matter in the form of the BBC micro:bit programmable device. Okay, so the micro:bit might not be a disruptive device in terms of consumer electronics, but it may well serve to disrupt the computing education market in the same way that the original BBC Micro classroom computer helped turn many UK kids into computer programmers.

I believe in the *Keep It Simple, Stupid* approach to just about everything. In this basic book I have kept it simple by focusing on the simplest version of the BBC micro:bit; the one that you can buy here from Amazon.co.uk at http://amzn.to/2aFFAHG. According to my *Just Enough Essential Parts (JEEP)* approach, all you will need in order to work with this book is a micro:bit plus a Windows PC and (optionally) an Android smartphone.

We won't be connecting the micro:bit up to a wide range additional sensors or input devices, so the more advanced electronics aficionados amongst you will have to wait for a subsequent book to take you beyond the basics.

As you work through the book you will notice that some text is **bold** (usually meaning that it refers to something you'll see on your screen) and some text is in an `alternative code font` (meaning something you will usually see in a code script).

About the Author

Allow me to introduce myself. I'm Tony, and I first got into computer programming during the personal computing heydays of the 1980s. In my teens I created computer games using everything from high level languages to low level machine code before doing a degree in computer science that led to a career in computing.

Over time I became less of a programmer and more of a software designer, analyst, course instructor and even an associate lecturer for the UK's Open University. I got into writing about computing first by contributing feature articles to online and print programming journals, and then by authoring and co-authoring books about computing.

After a slight detour into financial writing and freelance publishing consultancy, I returned to professional technical writing in 2015 and set about reacquainting myself with how to write code for computers. Yes, I was rather rusty, but I figured...

What could be better than the BBC micro:bit for re-learning the ropes and passing my newly-acquired knowledge on to you?

1 – All About the BBC Micro:Bit

The BBC micro:bit is the end result of a series of educational initiatives that began with the *Make It Digital* initiative. To set the scene, in this chapter I first present my interpretation of those initiatives. Then I describe the micro:bit device that defines the end result of those educational efforts.

BBC Takes the Technology Teaching Initiative (again)

The British Broadcasting Corporation (BBC) launched the UK-wide *Make It Digital* initiative to inspire a new generation of kids to create, code and program using digital technology. The aim of this project was to put digital creativity at the forefront and (once again) to help build the nation's digital skills through a range of programmes, partnerships and projects including:

- The BBC micro:bit microcomputer that would be given to all Year 7 schoolchildren across the UK.
- A series of digitally-inspirational BBC television and radio programmes.
- The *Make It Digital* traineeship for up to 5,000 unemployed people.
- Partnerships with 50+ organizations around the UK.
- A set of educational activities and events based around the BBC's Bitsize, Live Lessons and School Report programmes.

As someone who first became accustomed to computers in the 1980s, this all reminds me of something. It reminds me of the original *BBC Micro* classroom computer that was used extensively to teach computing in UK primary and secondary schools, and which inspired an entire generation of computer coders.

In some ways, the micro:bit seems like a step back even further, to the 1970s when very basic personal computers came as kits to be assembled by amateur engineers. But this approach doesn't seem so silly when we consider that the micro:bit follows in the wake of the superficially similar and very popular Raspberry Pi that took computing education very much back to basics.

In the years between the original BBC Micro and the BBC micro:bit, computing in UK schools had increasingly become more about consumption (of digital content) than coding. The micro:bit baulks this trend by going back to the basics of computer programming. And this time it's personal, because − unlike the original shared classroom computer − every schoolchild was set to get their very own micro:bit to use at home as well as at school.

Although the micro:bit is in some ways a throwback to the computer teaching of the past, it is also a thoroughly modern microcomputer that has more in common with your mobile phone. In this respect it sports an accelerometer (to monitor movement), a compass (to determine direction), and Bluetooth (to connect with other devices).

An important distinction between the micro:bit and the original BBC Micro is that latter was an all-in-one hardware + software solution: you used the built-in BBC BASIC programming language to control the very computer on which the code was created. In contrast, micro:bit code is created by accessing the BBC micro:bit web site via a PC, tablet or smartphone that is separate from the micro:bit itself. This is a good thing because the micro:bit 5 x 5 pixel matrix display would provide a very limited visual programming environment indeed.

About the Micro:Bit

The micro:bit is a credit card-sized computer circuit board that may variously be described as a microcomputer (it is micro in size, and it is a computer) or as a microcontroller (because you can connect it up to devices that you can control).

These days we are surrounded by microcontrollers that we simply don't see: in cars, consumer electronics, white goods like washing machines, office equipment and medical devices. If you opened up one of these devices, you might see something similar to the micro:bit, the whole purpose of which is to take some inputs (from buttons or sensors) and transform them into appropriate outputs (like status lights or moving motors). The transformation of inputs into outputs is performed by the program (or 'script' in micro:bit programming parlance) that runs or 'executes' on the microcontroller.

Anatomy of the Micro:Bit

Here I present the anatomy of the micro:bit (i.e. its constituent parts) as viewed from the front and from the back.

From the Front

The next picture shows what the micro:bit looks like from the front. The various parts are:

- The red **LEDs** (light emitting diodes) that form a 5 x 5 grid can be switched on and off programmatically to display patterns. *Note that there is also a yellow status LED on the back of the unit.*
- **BUTTON A** and **BUTTON B** can both be programmed to respond to being pressed (or released). *Note that there is also a reset button on the back of the unit that will restart and run your current*

downloaded program, or will send the unit into maintenance mode if pressed accidentally while connecting the USB.

- The large **I/O RINGS** for the pins 0-2 are where you can attach external sensors.
- The 3V and GND **POWER RINGS** or pins provide power to any external devices... as long as the micro:bit itself it powered by battery or by USB.

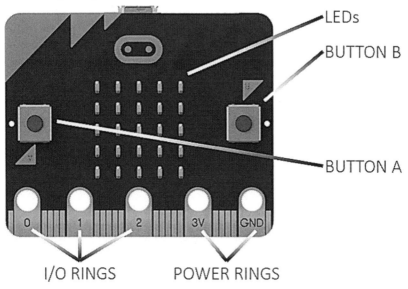

I/O RINGS   POWER RINGS

From the Back

This next picture shows what the micro:bit looks like from the back. The various parts are:

- The Bluetooth **ANTENNA** allows the micro:bit to communicate wirelessly with other devices such as smartphones and tablets.
- The **CPU** (Central Processing Unit) is the microchip that drives the micro:bit by executing (running) your programs. This is an ARM processor, similar to the one that probably powers your smartphone, and it is interesting to note that these ARM processors are designed by the company that was spun out from the company

(Acorn) that developed the original BBC Microcomputer all those years ago.

- The **MICRO-USB** socket is where you can attach a computer to the micro:bit using a USB cable, to transmit program data and to power the device.
- The **BATTERY CONNECTOR** is where you can attach a battery pack that holds two AAA batteries.
- The **ACCELEROMETER** detects if the micro:bit is being shaken, tilted... or dropped!
- The **COMPASS** can detect magnetic fields such as that of the Earth, and hence knows which way the micro:bit is moving plus which way it is facing.
- The small **EDGE PINS** that run along the bottom side of the micro:bit allow you to slot the device into an edge connector for greater input / output possibilities.

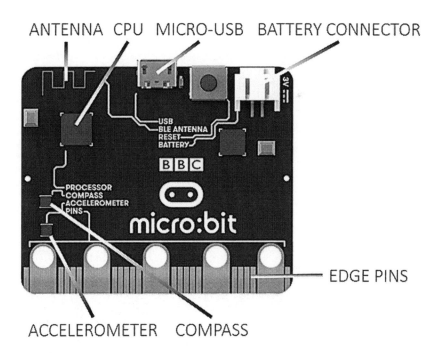

The low level language used to program the processor is called machine code, which is efficient but hard to learn. So in this book we'll use one or more high level languages.

What Did You Just Learn?

In this chapter you learned how the British Broadcasting Corporation (BBC) – in conjunction with Microsoft, Samsung and other organisations – once again took the technology teaching initiative with the micro:bit, some thirty years after doing something similar with the original BBC Micro personal computer. You also learned about the basic anatomy (the lights, buttons and other components) of the micro:bit hardware circuit board.

2 – Making the Micro:Bit Connection

Now that you know what the micro:bit is, how it originated, and what it looks like, it's time to talk about connecting it up with another device so that you can transfer programs. Except that this chapter is actually optional because you can follow my subsequent micro:bit coding tutorials without even owning a micro:bit.

If you do have a micro:bit, read on. If not, then you can safely skip ahead to the next chapter.

Connecting to a Computer via USB

Connecting to a Windows PC can be as simple as plugging one end of a USB cable into your computer, and the other end into the micro-USB socket on the micro:bit as shown in the previous picture. This is necessary not only so that you can transfer programs to the micro:bit, but also to power it if you do not have an attached battery pack.

When the micro:bit first powers up, you should find that via indicators on the display (such as **<-** and **->**) it invites you to perform some actions like pressing the two buttons in turn and then shaking the device.

You should also see that a new folder has appeared in your computer's File Explorer named **MICROBIT**, like this:

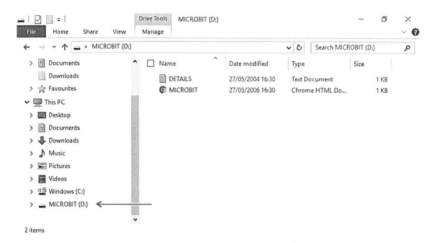

Clarification About Copying Compiled Code Files

Whenever you compile some code into a machine code **.hex** file using one of the online code editors (explained later) you are advised to copy the file onto this folder in order to run the program on the micro:bit. I have found this not to be necessary, since the compiled code seems to find its way onto the micro:bit without the need to copy it across.

However, if you obtain a compiled code **.hex** file by some other means – e.g. via email or by downloading it from a web site – then you will certainly need to copy it from your **Downloads** folder to the MICROBIT folder in order to execute it (i.e. run it) on the device.

Attaching to Android via Bluetooth using the Samsung App

You can download the Samsung app by visiting the Samsung web site at http://www.samsung.com/uk/microbit/ from your Android smartphone or tablet and choosing the **Get the App** option. Alternatively, you can simply search the Google Play app store for "samsung micro:bit".

Once you have enabled Bluetooth on your Android mobile device, pairing the device is achieved by working through the sequence of screens shown below, which appear in sequence once you have selected the **Connections** option on the main screen.

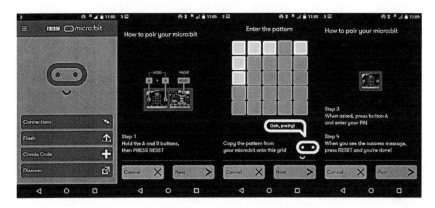

The pairing sequence is somewhat convoluted since it requires you to enter a pattern (which will appear at the right time on the micro:bit display) followed by a PIN (ditto), but you should only have to work through this pairing process once.

With your micro:bit connected to your Android device via Bluetooth, the code scripts that you create can henceforth be transferred to the micro:bit for execution (i.e. running the program) simply by selecting the **Flash** option as shown here:

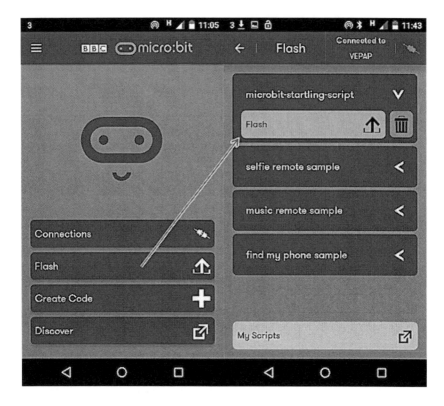

Create Code from Your Android Phone

In case you're wondering, I can tell you that the **Create Code** option on the app main screen takes you to the micro:bit web page where you can create code scripts using your choice of code editor. It's exactly the same web page (at https://www.microbit.co.uk/create-code) that you would visit to create code using your PC. Obviously this code-creating web page will be better viewed using a big-screen Android tablet rather than the small-screen Android smartphone that I used for convenience to produce the previous screenshots, but nonetheless I have found it perfectly possible to create code using the online editors accessed from an Android phone. And the advantage of accessing your created apps from your phone is that they can be tested by taking advantage of the phone's accelerometer and compass without even connecting to a micro:bit device.

What Did You Just Learn?

In this chapter you learned how to connect your micro:bit up to a personal computer via USB, or to an Android smartphone or tablet via the separate Samsung app. The USB option is necessary not only so that you can transfer compiled code to the micro:bit for execution, but also to power the micro:bit if you do not have a separate battery pack attached. The Samsung app option allows you to transfer compiled code to the micro:bit for execution, or to test it using your phone as a substitute for the micro:bit.

Research and Resources

You can learn more about the Samsung mobile app, the pairing process, and the resolutions to possible problems on the micro:bit web site at www.microbit.co.uk/mobile.

3 – Micro:Bit Computer Coding Quick-Start

When it comes to creating code for the micro:bit, you have a number of options that are accessible via the **Create Code** section of the BBC micro:bit web site at:

https://www.microbit.co.uk/create-code

At the time of writing, the options are **Code Kingdoms JavaScript**, the **Microsoft Block Editor**, **Microsoft Touch Develop**, and the **Python** programming language as shown here:

In this chapter we'll look at the easiest programming possibility that takes the form of the Microsoft Block Editor. The aim is to provide a quick-and-easy demonstration of how an example app can be coded, tested, compiled and transmitted to your micro:bit for execution.

Feel free to play along by reproducing these steps.

Microsoft Block Editor End-to-End Quick-Start Tutorial

The Block Editor is a visual editor that provides an introduction to structured programming via a drag-and-drop interface comprising coding blocks that snap together. To help with the transition to text-based programming, you can convert a Block Editor script into a Touch Develop script.

Step 1: Start a New Project

On the micro:bit **Create Code** web page at www.microbit.co.uk/create-code, locate the Microsoft Block Editor and select the **New project** option:

A graphical, drag and drop code editor, where coding blocks snap together.

New project ←——————————

Follow Tutorial

Tell me more about this editor

⊟ Editor documentation

Step 2: Add an Input Block

The Block Editor coding canvas will appear as shown in the next picture. To the right of the canvas you will see an emulation of the micro:bit front panel that allows you to see your results without even owning a micro:bit at all. To the left of the canvas you will see a list of available blocks, arranged into categories, which can be moved onto the canvas by clicking (hold down the left mouse button – or equivalent) and dragging them (move the mouse cursor with the button still held down).

In the following picture I have dragged an **on button A pressed do** block from the **Input** category onto the canvas.

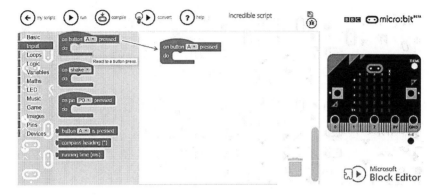

Computers are all about inputs and outputs—you provide some input, and the computer produces some output in response. In this case our input will be the pressing of Button A.

Step 3: Add an Output Block

Now it's time to add the corresponding output for this input. I do this by dragging the **show string "Hello!"** block from the **Basic** category until it clicks into place within our already-placed input block:

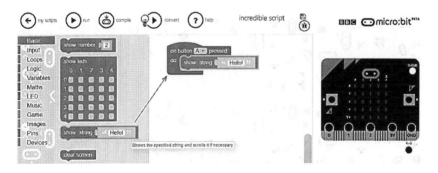

I then type new text within the text box of the new block, to read "Ouch!" rather than "Hello!".

The reason for me changing this text is not only to show you how to do it, but because it's a little more fun for the computer to say "Ouch!" when you press one of its buttons. Or at least I thought so 35 years ago when the demonstration program for my first ever computer (the Sinclair ZX81) did exactly this.

Step 4: Run (and Test) the Script

You can run (or "execute") the program script defined by this set of blocks by clicking the **run** icon at the top of the screen. Then, whenever you click the screen representation of Button A on the micro:bit emulator, you will see that the message "Ouch!" scrolls across the screen composed of the 5 x 5 LEDs.

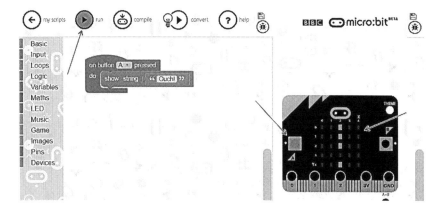

Step 5: Compile the Code for the Micro:Bit

In order to run this program on a real micro:bit you need to compile the code into micro:bit machine code, which you can do simply by clicking the **compile** icon at the top of the screen. Once the compilation has completed, a message will appear to advise you that...

```
"Your .hex file is ready. Drag and drop it onto your BBC
micro:bit device drive."
```

Note: I have found this step of copying the .hex file onto the micro:bit device drive usually to be unnecessary. The compile option itself will transfer the code to the micro:bit for execution.

Having done this, you can now run and test the functionality on the micro:bit in exactly the same way as you did using the emulator: just press Button A to see the micro:bit say "Ouch!".

Oh, and if you're wondering what a .hex file looks like, it's a series of base-16 hexadecimal digits (hence hex) that encode the machine code instructions for your program. And it looks like this (cut short); the incomprehensibility of which serves to illustrate the need for high level programming languages like Python and high level code creation tools like the Microsoft Block Editor:

```
:020000040000FA
:10000000C0070000D1060000D1000000B1060000CA
:1000100000000000000000000000000000000000E0
:10002000000000000000000000000000005107000078
:100030000000000000000000DB000000E500000000
:10004000EF000000F9000000301000000D010000B6
:100050001701000021010002B010000350100004
:100060003F010000490100005301000005D0100054
:10007000670100007101000007B01000085010000A4
:100080008F01000099010000A3010000AD010000F4
:10009000B7010000C1010000CB010000D501000044
:1000A000DF010000E9010000F3010000FD01000094
:1000B000070200001102000001B0200002502020000E0
:1000C0001FB5C046C04600F0EFFA04B00FB41FBD24
...
```

Step 6: Convert to Code (Optional)

Remember I told you that one of the features of the Block Editor was to convert the graphical block arrangements into something resembling proper program code? The purpose of this optional step is to do exactly that by clicking the **convert** icon at the top of the Block Editor screen:

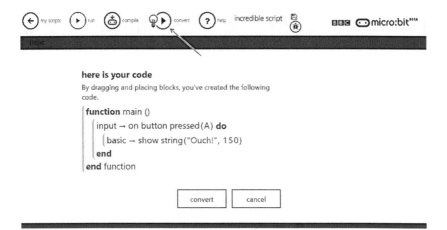

The end result is to take you out of the Microsoft Block Editor and into the Microsoft Touch Develop environment that looks like this:

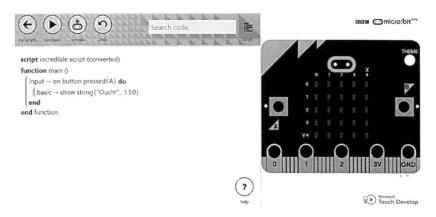

The good news is that even with this conversion of blocks to code, we're still working at a much higher level than the hexadecimal machine code shown earlier.

Tony's To-Dos

If you played along by reproducing my steps yourself, you might now like to experiment by adapting the simple script. Some specific simple things you might try are:

- Changing the program to respond to Button B rather than Button A.
- Using the **show leds** block rather than the show **string block**, to present your own pattern – how about a sad face? – rather than a scrolling message.

What Did You Just Learn?

In this chapter you learned that the BBC micro:bit web site offers a variety of graphical and textual programming possibilities to suit all skill levels. Using the Microsoft Block Editor, you learned how to compose some simple code graphically to produce some output ("Ouch!") in response to some input (the Button A pressed event). This code was tested using the on-screen emulator, was compiled for transferring to real micro:bit device, and was converted into the equivalent Microsoft Touch Develop textual code script.

From a programming perspective, you learned about an **event** (the button being pressed) and a **string** (a sequence or alphanumeric characters that for a word or sentence).

Research and Resources

You can learn a little more about the Block Editor by watching the online video located at:

www.microbit.co.uk/getting-started/block-editor

You can learn a little more about the Touch Develop Editor by watching the online video located at:

www.microbit.co.uk/getting-started/touchdevelop-editor

4 – A Short Journey into JavaScript

Before we dig any deeper into coding constructs and controls using the Microsoft Block Editor and Microsoft Touch Develop, let me first lure you into considering coding in JavaScript instead—just so you know what you would be dealing with if you did decide to go down the alternative JavaScript route.

If you're really not interested in programming the micro:bit using JavaScript, you can safely skip ahead to the next chapter.

JavaScript End-to-End Quick-Start Tutorial

Feel free to play along by reproducing these steps.

Step 1: Start a New Project

On the micro:bit **Create Code** web page at www.microbit.co.uk/create-code, locate the JavaScript editor and select the **New project** option:

Step 2: Compose the Code

We'll take the previous chapter's "Ouch!" example a stage further by responding to more events than simply the pressing of Button A. We'll also respond to the shaking of the device and to the event that signals the start of the program. In fact, let's start with `onStart()`.

The onStart() Event

As soon as the editor opens, you should see the `onStart()` function that gets triggered when the program starts. In the following picture I have dragged the `draw(Pattern)` function from the list on the left to within the body of the `onStart()` function. I am then able to substitute the `Pattern` of my choice by clicking the down-arrow to display the dropdown list of options.

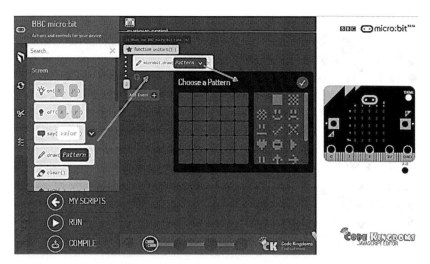

I choose the smiley face, which will now appear in the emulator (as shown below) whenever this program is run.

The onShake() and onPressA() Events

Now it's time for the main events. I click the **Add Event +** icon to bring up a list of new events, and I choose the one named `onShake()`.

33

I repeat this this process so that there is also an `onPressA()` event, and I complete the code by dragging a `draw(Pattern)` function onto each of the two new events so that shaking the device draws a sad face ("Ouch!") and pressing Button A returns the micro:bit to its happy state with a happy face. It's all shown here:

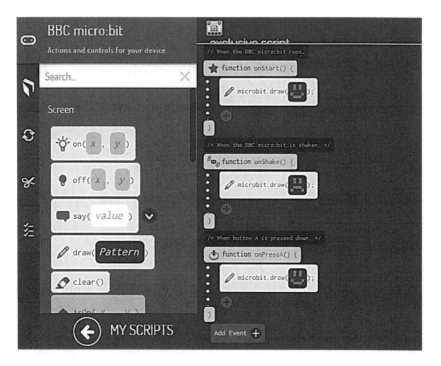

What to Do When You Make a Mistake

If you're playing along by attempting to reproduce these steps for yourself, you might find yourself frustrated when you accidentally drag the wrong function onto the canvas from the list on the left.

Don't Panic!

At any time, you can click-and-hold once of the functions on the canvas and drag it to the trash can that appears. Like this:

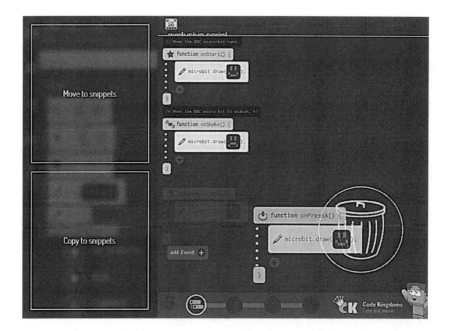

Step 3: Testing the Program

You can test this program by clicking the **RUN** button at the left side of the screen and clicking the **SHAKE** button on the emulator at the right side of the screen.

You can also test this code by clicking the **COMPILE** button at the left of the screen to compile a machine code **.hex** file to be copied onto you micro:bit drive, exactly like you did in the previous chapter.

Note again that I have found the separate copy step to be unnecessary since the code seems to copy to the micro:bit automatically once it has compiled.

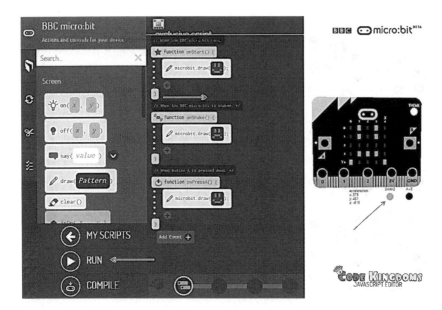

The micro:bit in its two states (sad and happy again) will look like this:

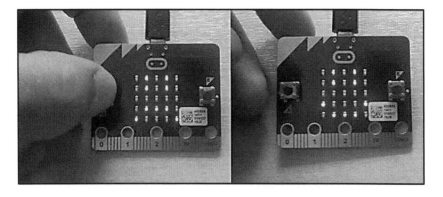

Step 4: Convert to Code (Optional)

As with the Microsoft Block Editor which allows you to convert the graphical blocks representation of your program into something more closely resembling 'proper' code script, this JavaScript editor allows you to do something very similar but without a separate step.

At any point you can click the circles (see below) at the bottom of the screen to see the various representations of your code, each one less graphical and more textual.

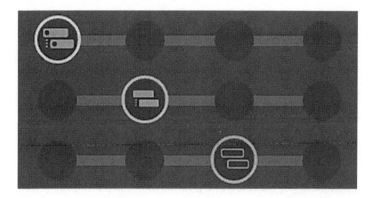

The logical conclusion to this is the most code-like textual code representation that looks like this:

```
1  // when the BBC micro:bit runs.
2  function onStart( ) {
3      microbit.draw(Pattern("01010.01010.00000.10001.01110")
4
5  }
6
7  function onShake( ) {
8      microbit.draw(Pattern("01010.01010.00000.01110.10001")
9
10 }
11
12 function onPressA( ) {
13     microbit.draw(Pattern("01010.01010.00000.10001.01110")
14
15 }
16
```

var x

CK Code Kingdoms
Find out more

It's exactly the same program; just a different way of looking at it.

Tony's To-Dos

If you played along by reproducing my steps yourself, you might now like to experiment by adapting the simple script in the final code view shown above. You should see how the sequences of 1s and 0s correspond with the happy and sad face patterns that are displayed in response to the buttons presses, and you could change these binary strings ("1" for on, and 0 for "off") to display an alternative pattern of your choice. How about encoding a cross and a square like the ones shown in binary below?

```
10001    11111
01010    10001
00100    10001
01010    10001
10001    11111
```

What Did You Just Learn?

In this chapter you learned how to compose some simple micro:bit code graphically using the Code Kingdoms JavaScript Editor. This program took my "Ouch!" idea a little further by responding to more events and by displaying images rather than a scrolling message on the micro:bit display.

From a programming point of view you also learned how the pattern of lit and unlit LEDs on the micro:bit matrix can be represented as a set of binary numbers with "1" meaning "on" and "0" meaning "off".

I won't pursue JavaScript any further in this book for two reasons:

- It's beyond the scope of this basic book that concentrates on the Microsoft Block Editor and Microsoft Touch Develop.
- JavaScript is a well-established programming language, which you will either know already or which you can learn from one of the many books dedicated solely to the subject.

Research and Resources

You can learn a little more about the Code Kingdoms JavaScript Editor by reading the PDF located at:

www.microbit.co.uk/getting-started/code-kingdoms

And you can learn even more by reading the PDF located at:

microbit0.blob.core.windows.net/pub/zgqksajs/BBC-microbit-Code-Kingdoms-Cookbook.pdf

5 – A Python Primer

You should know the routine by now. In this chapter we will do almost exactly the same thing for the Python programming language that we did for JavaScript and the earlier Microsoft Block Editor / Touch Develop combo: creating some code to be taken all the way to the micro:bit device in quick-start fashion. It's what I'm calling "a Python primer", and it's where we start to get serious about writing code—but not too serious!

If you're really not interested in programming the micro:bit using Python, you can safely skip ahead to the next chapter.

The version of Python that runs on the BBC micro:bit is called MicroPython.

Python End-to-End Quick-Start Tutorial

Feel free to play along by reproducing these steps.

Step 1: Start a New Project

On the micro:bit **Create Code** web page at www.microbit.co.uk/create-code, locate the Python entry and select the **New project** option:

An easy-to-learn programming language for everyone, from kids to teachers to professional software engineers.

New project ←——————————

Tell me more about this editor

Editor documentation

Step 2: Type the Python Program Code

The Python editor will appear, and you can enter the code for one of the simplest possible Python programs as shown below. This script does something quite similar to (but not the same as) the previous chapter's JavaScript script. In this case it displays a "happy face" image on the LED matrix, which changes to a sad face (ouch!) whenever Button A is pressed... and reverts to the happy face when the button is released. When Button B is pressed, the program ends.

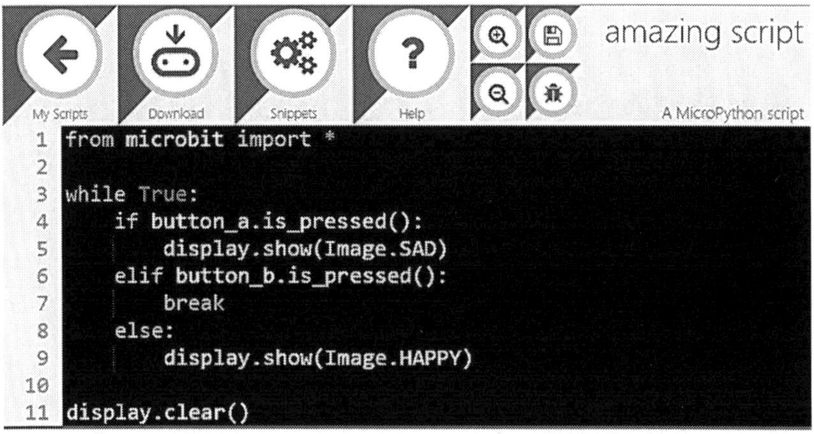

```
amazing script
A MicroPython script
1  from microbit import *
2
3  while True:
4      if button_a.is_pressed():
5          display.show(Image.SAD)
6      elif button_b.is_pressed():
7          break
8      else:
9          display.show(Image.HAPPY)
10
11 display.clear()
```

The complete code is listed below, so that you can copy and paste it into the editor if you are reading this book electronically.

```
from microbit import *

while True:
    if button_a.is_pressed():
        display.show(Image.SAD)
    elif button_b.is_pressed():
        break
    else:
        display.show(Image.HAPPY)

display.clear()
```

What's it All About, Tony?

The lines of code that are numbered in the original screenshot perform the following functions:

#1: This line tells MicroPython to import all ("*") of the supporting code libraries (without which the program won't work) from the microbit module.

#2: Blank line.

#3: This line tells MicroPython to keep looping (i.e. repeatedly running the subsequent code) while the statement is true. Since the statement True will always be true, it will keep looping forever until the loop is broken.

#4: This line is a conditional statement that tells MicroPython to execute the next line "if" Button A is being pressed.

#5: If the previous condition is satisfied because Button A is being pressed, then we show the SAD image on the micro:bit display.

#6: If the previous condition on line #3 fails, we immediately test another condition to see if Button B is currently being pressed.

#7: If the previous condition is satisfied because Button B is being pressed, we break the loop to end the program.

#8: If the previous two conditions have failed because no button is currently being pressed, then if all else fails…

#9: We show the HAPPY face on the micro:bit display. Thus the happy face will always be on display (every time around the loop) until the program receives some input.

#10: Blank line.

#11: When the loop is broken and the program is about to end, we tell MicroPython to clear the micro:bit display.

Step 3: Download to the Device

The MicroPython editor has no on-screen emulator, so in this case we have no choice but to download the code to the device for testing.

Simply clicking the **Download** icon at the top of the screen should download the compiled script to the micro:bit device... with no need to copy the .hex file manually into the device folder.

Step 4: The Python Program in Action

Since this Python program displays the same two images as the previous JavaScript one, the "in action" photographs are essentially the same:

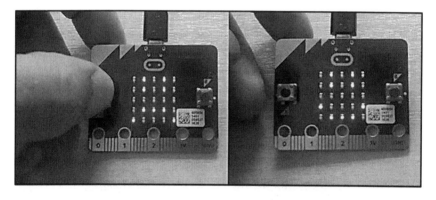

Tony's To-Dos

If you played along by reproducing my steps yourself, you might now like to experiment by adapting the simple script to reverse the sense of the happy and sad patterns. What I mean is... to make the SAD state the default state so that the operator can make the micro:bit HAPPY by pressing the button.

What Did You Just Learn?

In this chapter we implemented similar functionality of the previous JavaScript program, but this time using the Python programming language—the editor for which has no graphical code composition option. In some senses, this is more like what professional computer programmers would do.

The program included a *(while) loop* and an *(if) condition*, and you had to transfer the compiled program direct to the micro:bit for testing because there is no emulator.

From a programming point of view, this program was subtly different from what went before. Whereas the previous program in JavaScript was "event-driven" because it actively responded when electronic messages signalled that buttons had been pressed, this program wasn't event driven because we passively tested the current button state(s) while looping infinitely.

I won't pursue Python any further in this book for two reasons:

- It's beyond the scope of this basic book that concentrates on the Microsoft Block Editor and Microsoft Touch Develop.
- Python is a well-established programming language, which you will either know already or which you can learn from one of the many books dedicated solely to the subject.

Research and Resources

You can learn a little more about the Python editor by watching the online video located at www.microbit.co.uk/getting-started/python#.

Want to know more about programming the micro:bit with Python? You will find an excellent set of tutorials – including one very similar to this example – on the MicroPython web site at microbit-micropython.readthedocs.io/en/latest/tutorials/introduction.html.

6 – Working with the Web Site and Block Editor

While I wanted to get you going with some simple scripts in the various code editors, it's now time to go back to basics by learning more about working with code scripts in general on the micro:bit web site. Then we'll dig a little deeper into the workings of the Block Editor that will underpin the subsequent coding case studies.

Finding Your Way Around the Web Site

Across the top of the BBC micro:bit web site at www.microbit.co.uk you will find the following links:

Create Code – which we will explore in depth in the rest of this book.

About – which tells you a little more about the micro:bit itself, and which leads off to some additional pages...such as the hardware page that tells you a lot more about the device details.

Getting Started – which links to instructional videos that will put you on the path to progress with the micro:bit.

Teachers and Parents – which contains a collection of lessons, lectures, videos and other resources that will help you make even more micro:bit progress. It's pretty much everything you could ever need to know.

Help – which presents an alphabetical list of help topics, and which offers additional help by email. According to the web site, the BBC micro:bit team is "happy to help".

You will also see a link to My Scripts, which takes you to your (not my) list of auto-saved code scripts. This leads us naturally on to...

Working Without Signing-In

It is perfectly possible to write code scripts in the online code editors at www.microbit.co.uk/create-code without ever setting up an account and signing in. As long as you use the same computer each time, your scripts will be saved and listed for your convenience the next time you log in. Since you created some scripts in previous chapters, you should see something like this when you click the My Scripts link at the top-right of the micro:bit web site:

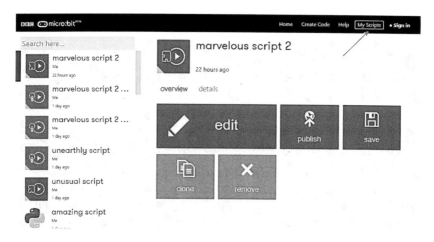

Down the left-hand side you can see the scripts you have worked on in the different code editors, and you can use the buttons to the right to **edit** a specific script or perform additional actions such as **save** the script to your current computer.

While the web site remembers the scripts you have been working on, this is per-device, so when logging in from your smartphone you won't see the scripts you created using the web browser on your PC.

One way of getting a script from one device to another is to save the script from Device #1 and then (after emailing it to yourself or saving in shared location) import it from Device #2.

Save the script from one device:

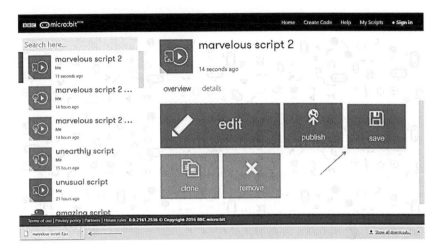

Import it from another device:

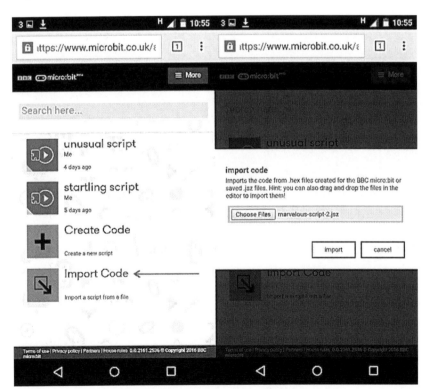

I did this several times in the course of constructing the following case studies, so that – for example – I could build a Block Editor solution using my PC but then test it using my Android mobile phone.

Signing-In and Publishing Scripts

The other way to make your scripts available on all your devices is to sign in to the micro:bit web site and publish your scripts. But that's not as simple as it might seem.

Students are discouraged, if not prevented, from signing-in. And teachers not only need an established online account (Office 365, Microsoft or Facebook) with which to sign in, but also need an authorisation code that should have been sent out with the students' microbits. Without this code it is not possible to publish student scripts.

What's the bottom line?

The bottom line is that as an ordinary user of the BBC micro:bit web site, you probably won't be required or even able to sign in. So in this book, we'll continue to work as though you won't.

Block Editor Basics

Since the remainder of the examples in this book will be based on the basic Block Editor, it's worth now setting out some of the Block Editor basics that we help you reproduce my results. Here is the basic anatomy of the Block Editor:

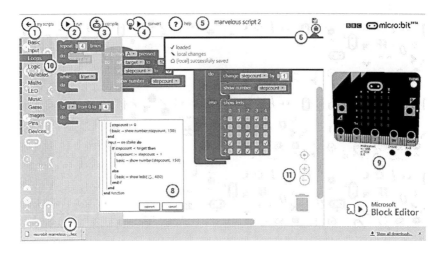

The **my scripts** button **(1)** takes you back to the list of scripts shown in the previous pictures.

The **run** button **(2)** runs the current script code in the on-screen emulator **(9)**. Note that the emulator has A and B buttons that can be pressed, plus an additional on-screen selector to simulate the pushing of both buttons A + B, plus an additional on-screen selector to simulate the shaking of the device. For programs that query the compass, you will see an additional directional indicator and control.

The **compile button (3)** compiles the current blocks arrangement into code that can be copied to a micro:bit device folder as a .hex file **(7)**, to be executed (i.e. run) on the device.

The **convert** button **(4)** converts the blocks representation of the code into a code script **(8)** that can be opened in the Microsoft Touch Develop Editor.

The next part of the button bar **(5)** at the top of the screen contains a **help** button alongside the name of your current code script. *You can click the script name in order to change it from the auto-generated name to a name of your choice.*

To the right of the script name **(6)** is a save indicator that looks like a floppy disc and a small bug icon that displays a transcript of the save status. Note that your work will be saved periodically, automatically, on-line.

Bock Editor code is composed by dragging individual blocks from sections of the block libraries **(10)** and assembling them like Lego bricks on the main canvas.

The canvas also has a set of buttons **(11)** at the bottom-right to respectively: centre the blocks on screen, zoom in and out, and bin any selected blocks (by dragging then into the bin).

Tony's To-Dos

In terms of to-dos, you my like to try your hand at practicing what I have preached by composing some code from one device and then saving the script to be imported via another device. And then simply get to grips with the Block Editor user interface by pushing the various buttons to see what they do.

What Did You Just Learn?

In this chapter I familiarised you with the BBC micro:bit web site. You learned about how scripts are saved when you're not signed-in, along with how to see the same scripts when accessing the web site from different devices. Then you learned about the basic anatomy of the Block Editor that will help you in the course of the case studies that follow.

7 – Compass Case Study for Conditional Logic

I'm a very practical and pragmatic person, and I believe that coding examples should have practical purposes rather than representing only abstract ideas. Despite its simplicity, the micro:bit actually lends itself to some very practical applications, the first of which we will explore in this *compass case study*. But in the course of the case study we will put into practice the abstract coding ideas associated with *conditional logic*.

What's the Problem?

The problem I want to solve is that of getting my micro:bit to display the correct compass reading (N, E, S, W) according to which way it is pointing.

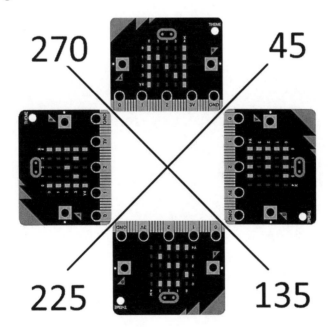

In this context I define...

- "N" as any direction greater than 270 degrees or less than 45 degrees from magnetic north.
- "E" as any direction between 45 degrees and 135 degrees from magnetic north.
- "S" as any direction between 135 degrees and 225 degrees from magnetic north.
- "W" as any direction between 225 degrees and 270 degrees from magnetic north.

What's the Solution?

The complete coded solution that I devised using the Block Editor is shown below. It was created by dragging various blocks from the list of libraries on the left, and assembling them on the canvas as shown. In a nutshell: the program loops forever (while true), and each time around the loop the compass heading is tested to see whether we should display N, E, S or W on the micro:bit display.

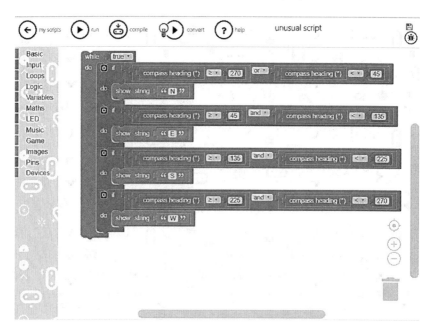

The Conditional Logic

In order to recreate my solution, you will need to refer to the following shopping list of **Logic** blocks.

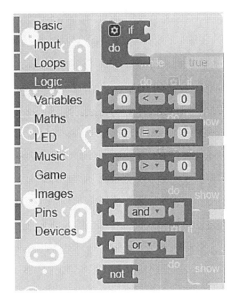

The **if...do** block executes the contained block if a particular condition is **true**.

These conditions are **true** if the left value is less than (<) or equal to (=) or greater than (>) the right value.

The **and** operator is true if both its operands (e.g. the conditions above) are **true**. The **or** operator is **true** if either of its operands are **true**.

The First Condition

In my sample solution, the first conditional statement is composed from these blocks – plus the **compass heading** block from the **Input** library, and the **show string** block from the **Basic** library – as follows:

The **if** condition is met (i.e. true), and therefore the single-letter string "N" is displayed if...

...the **compass heading** is **greater than or equal to** 270 degrees or the **compass heading** is **less than** 45 degrees.

Note the use of the compound ≥ (greater than or equal to) condition. We can't use only > (greater than) and < (less than) conditions because these would not account for the cases where the compass heading is exactly 45 degrees or 135 degrees or 225 degrees or 270 degrees.

The Second Condition

The second condition that displays "E" for East is very similar to the first one:

The notable difference this time is the use of the **and** operator rather than the **or** operator. Whereas a compass reading of ≥ 270 degrees **or** < 45 degrees (but mathematically it can't be both) indicates North, a compass reading of ≥ 45 degrees **and** < 135 degrees (and mathematically it must be both) indicates East.

The Third and Fourth Conditions

The third and fourth conditions are exactly the same as the third **and** condition, but with different degrees to indicate different directions.

Testing the Solution

Upon running the compass code, the result in the on-screen micro:bit emulator should look like this:

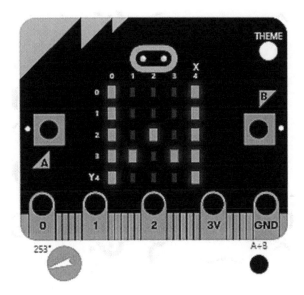

Note that the directional indicator at the bottom-left of the emulator can be rotated using the mouse cursor to see how the screen display responds. In this case a compass reading of 253 degrees correctly shows the approximate direction as "W" for West.

Making It Mobile

You might be interested to know that I constructed this micro:bit application originally by accessing the Block Editor from my Android smartphone. The following picture shows the blocks being assembled on the phone screen (to the left) with the corresponding converted code shown to the right.

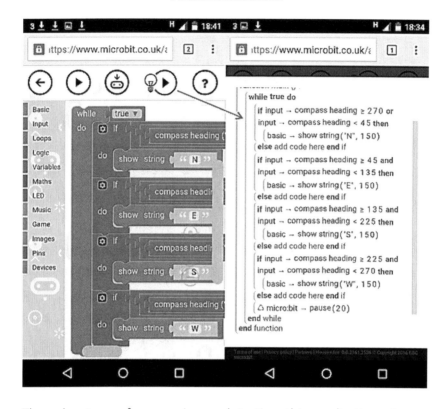

The advantage of composing and testing this application via my smartphone rather than within a PC web browser is that the phone'micro:bit emulator could detect the direction in which the phone's built-in compass was pointing without having to manually set the direction using an on-screen control. Simply by pointing the phone in different directions, I could obtain the following readings:

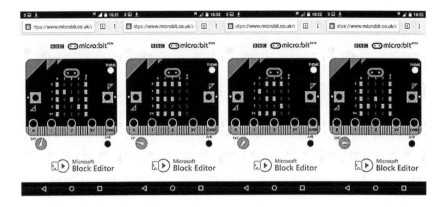

Tony's To-Dos

Now it's time for you "to do". After recreating my sample solution in the Block Editor, you might like to try your hand at the following additional tasks:

- Compile the code to be run on the micro:bit device itself rather than in the emulator.
- Adjust the existing conditions, and add four new ones, so that the display shows additional directions NE/SE/SW/NW in addition to the existing N/S/E/W. *Hint: NE will be deduced from a compass reading between 22.5 degrees and 67.5 degrees.*

What Did You Just Learn?

In this case study you learned a little more about the *conditional logic* that underpins computer programming. You learned how "Boolean" conditions (but I didn't tell you that's what they were) can resolve to **true** (rather than false) and how these can be used as a basis for making if-based decisions; in this case the decision about which directional letter to display on the LED matrix.

Note that from a programming point of view, this code did not necessarily represent best practice. Rather than testing the `compass` `heading` multiple times, it would have been better to store the current compass heading in a variable (see next chapter) and then to test the value of this variable within each condition.

Research and Resources

After devising this case study as an entirely original example (or so I thought), I subsequently saw that Dogan Ibrahim had implemented something very similar in his book "BBC micro:bit 27 Projects for Students Level 1" available at http://amzn.to/2baIUhC. Luckily for me, no one can copyright an idea (only the expression of that idea), so as long as I used different text and pictures to describe the idea... I'm in the clear! But it was only fair for me to acknowledge the existence of Dogan's alternative explanation.

8 – Step Counter Case Study for Variable Values

In this second micro:bit case study we will devise a coded solution that once again gives the device a very practical purpose. But besides this practical purpose, the case study obviously also has a programming objective—which in this case is to learn about program *variables* and the *values* they hold.

What's the Problem?

It seems that everyone is fanatical about fitness these days, and we are all encouraged to walk or run a certain number of steps every day. You may well have been encouraged to "take steps" towards better health by using a pedometer or step-counter (or equivalent smartphone app) to tell you how much you run, walk or jump during a typical day. We can put our micro:bit devices to exactly the same use by taking advantage of the fact that we can see when they have been shaken.

For the purposes of this case study, we will assume that *1 shake* equals *1 step* which should be accurate enough if you somehow attach your micro:bit to your leg or foot.

What's the Solution?

Now let's look at my solution to the step counting problem. First I'll show the solution built out of blocks, and then I'll explain why in this case I prefer the Touch Editor conversion of the code.

Building the Solution with Blocks

You should know by now how to drag blocks from the libraries at the side of the screen, and how to assemble them on the canvas. So in this case I'll simply show the end result for you to reproduce:

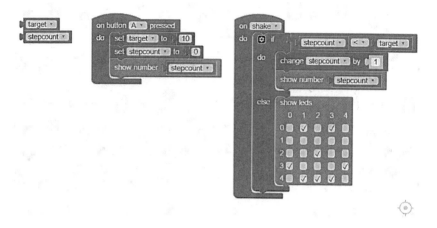

The Variables

On second thoughts, the first part of this solution does demand some demonstration in terms of creating the variables that underpin the program. The following screenshot shows how to create a new variable (which is basically a named storage unit for a value) by clicking the **item** block from the **Variables** library and then choosing the **New variable** option. We need to create two variables, named stepcount and target respectively.

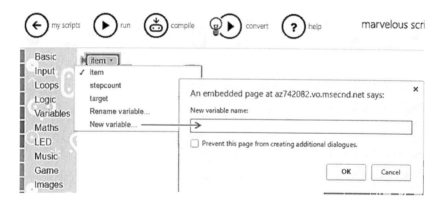

Starting the Step Count

In this solution, when Button A is pressed (on button A pressed) we start the step count (set stepcount to 0), we set the target (set `target to 10`), and we display the initial step count of 0. The user can restart the count at any time by pressing the button.

This shows the setting of variables to values (0 and 10 respectively), and in this case I have chosen a modest target of 10 steps rather than the recommended 10,000 steps per day simply because 10,000 steps would take too long to test.

Shake, Rattle and Roll

When the micro:bit is shaken (`on shake`) to simulate a step, we then test the condition to determine **if** the `stepcount` is still below the `target`.

If this test condition is true, we `change stepcount by 1` (increase the value held in the variable) and show the value of the `stepcount` variable on the LED display.

Else (if the test condition is not true), the step count must have reached the target so we show a smiley face on the LEDs.

Since it might not be obvious how to include the `else` clause in the if block after dragging it onto the canvas, I'll show you that you do it like this:

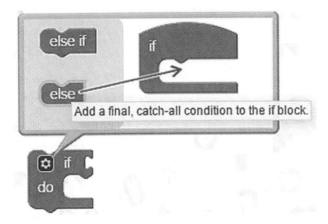

The Equivalent Touch Develop Code

In this case I think that the program logic is actually easier to understand by reading the equivalent Touch Develop code (see below) that can be obtained by clicking the **Convert** button at the top of the Block Editor screen, but this may well be because I have read and written code in a previous life.

```
script marvelous script 2 (converted) 2
function main ()
  var stepcount := 0
  var target := 0
  input → on button pressed(A) do
    target := 10
    stepcount := 0
    basic → show number(stepcount, 150)
  end
  input → on shake do
    if stepcount < target then
      stepcount := stepcount + 1
      basic → show number(stepcount, 150)
    else
      basic → show leds( ⬚ , 400)
    end if
  end
end function
```

One thing that this equivalent code does do is allow us to identify and fix a failing (let's call it a bug) in the original program.

The source of this bug is based on the fact that if the steps are taken quicker than the LED screen can show them, the display has to "catch up" by showing the missed steps before showing the smiley face when the stepcount target is reached.

As you should see in the code, this is because each of the numbers is set to show for 150 milliseconds, with the final smiley face set to show for 400 milliseconds. So the program can be made to behave better by ratcheting down those numbers to just 1 millisecond in the Touch Develop Editor. Like this:

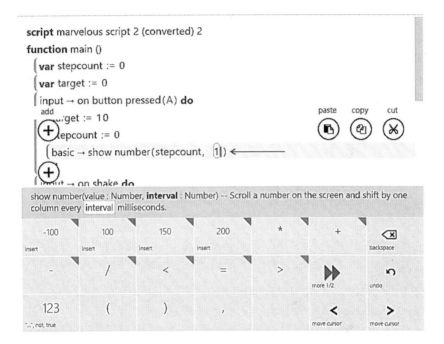

Testing, Testing

The following screenshots show what this application looks like when tested on an Android smartphone, which is my preferred testing vehicle because you can simply shake the phone to simulate the steps. Note that if running the tests on a traditional PC you would need to click the **SHAKE** button (indicated below) to simulate a step.

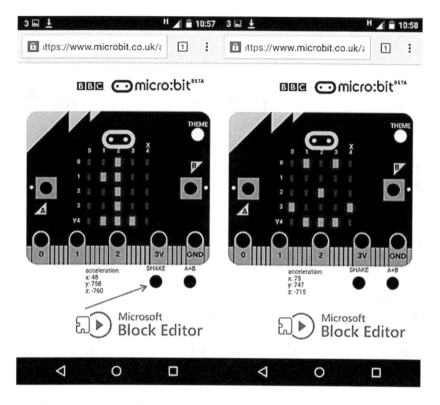

Another way you might try to test this program is to tape your micro:bit to your shoe as shown below, and take it for a walk or a run. You'd need the battery pack attached (not shown), and you'd have to be very careful with this one because you don't want to damage the device!

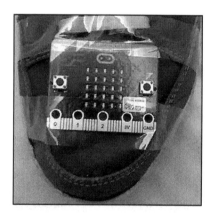

Tony's To-Dos

In this case I really can't think of anything you can do to improve or adapt the code... apart from changing the starting value of the `target` variable from `10` to a more realistic `10000`. But you have plenty to be getting on with by reproducing my arrangement of blocks, converting to Touch Develop code, compiling the code, and testing it on your micro:bit.

What Did You Just Learn?

In this chapter you learned how to store values in variables, which when written in code uses the assignment operator (:=) that should not be confused with the 'equals' operator (=) which tests equality. In other words, there is a big difference between...

`Stepcount := 0` (assignment)

and (for example) ...

`if stepcount = 10` (equality comparison)

In the program, we actually did a slightly different comparison between two variables:

`if stepcount < target`

You also learned a little more about event-driven programming, though I didn't call it that. This means writing a program that just sits around doing nothing until it is time to react to an event such as pressing a button or shaking the device.

Research and Resources

As with my previous compass case study, I thought I'd been entirely original here. That is, until I saw a similar app described at https://www.microbit.co.uk/iet/stepometer. The good news for you is that you can get a second bite at this cherry by checking out the alternative implementation to see how it compares with mine.

9 – Pin Programming Case Study

While I never promised any exploration of electronics in this book, it would be remiss of me not to mention the possibility of programming the micro:bit pins, so I'll show in principle how you can give those pins a purpose. The whole point of the pins is to allow to you to connect your micro:bit with other electronic equipment that you can control or take readings from.

From a programming point of view, in this chapter you'll learn something about the different between binary *digital* data and continuously varying *analog* data.

Pin Input

For the first part of this case study, I searched high and low around my house to find something (anything) that I could plausibly use as some kind of switch to provide input to my micro:bit. What I found was a magnetic contact switch that came as part of a self-install home alarm system, plus some old coaxial cable with which to connect it up to my micro:bit.

My basic setup (shown above) is by no means a good example of electronic engineering.

In this very simple setup I attached the two wires at one end of my cable to the two connectors on the magnetic switch, and the two wires at the other end of the cable to the micro:bit pins labelled **2** and **GND**. In general, when programming with pins, you will always connect one wire to GND (which means "ground", or what my dad would have called "earth") and the other wire to the particular pin you wish to program.

As you may already have imagined, my objective was to simulate some kind of alarm system that would trigger (as though a door had been opened) when the magnetics moved together or apart. My very basic Block Editor program, which simply displays an "X" when it receives some kind of input from the switch connected to PIN 2 (**P2**) is shown here:

I'm sure I don't need to tell you, by now, how to compile this code for execution on the micro:bit itself. So I won't, and I'll assume you know how to do it if you decide to.

Although in practice this home-made alarm system turned out to react in a rather hit-and-miss fashion, you can see from my earlier picture that I did get it to work at least once. I have to say, though, that I achieved somewhat better success by doing away with the magnetic switch and simply touching the wires together.

Pin Output

Pins can provide output signals as well as read input signals. So in my second set-up I simply switched my input switch for some output headphones connected rather haphazardly as you can see in the picture. In this case, the micro:bit connections remained the same.

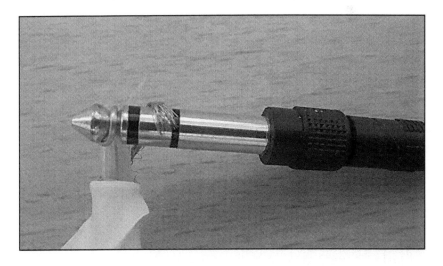

No, I'm not looking to win any electronics awards here. I'm just setting out to see if I can elicit any kind of output from a micro:bit pin using the most basic equipment. I'm not looking to win any programming awards either, since I have devised the simplest possible program here to test the output to PIN 2:

And the amazing output from this program when I'm wearing the attached headphones? Just a subtle – but very noticeable – "click" when the compiled script starts.

No Electronics Needed

Yes, I know these have been very simple examples of programming with pins, but bear in mind that this is a basic book. So I basically just wanted to go through the motions of connecting the micro:bit pins to very basic input and output devices; devices that I found lying around my house.

In practice, I probably wouldn't suggest connecting up your micro:bit pins at all if you merely want to play with the principles of responding to simple pin "presses". To some extent you can do this entirely in the emulator by (for example) pressing the on-screen pins. Like this:

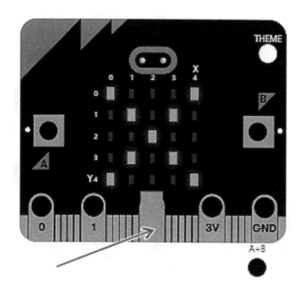

Tony's To-Dos

Maybe you have a similar switch lying somewhere around your home. Maybe you have a spare set of headphones and some simple cable to connect them up to your micro:bit. In which case your first *to-do* could be to do what I just did, to test the basic operation of your micro:bit pins.

Your second *to-do* could be to make the move from digital to analog electronics...

From Digital to Analog

In this case study I have dealt only with digital data. Either the pin is pressed (**1**) or it isn't (**0**); either headphones make a click (**1**) or they don't (**0**). In the real world outside of computers, things are not so binary black-and-white, they're more "analog"—which means a continuous range of values that vary according to the strength of the input.

So your mission (should you choose to accept it) is to take another simple script like this one...

...and test it by doing various things with the two ends of wire that are not connected to the micro:bit. You might try touching the two ends together, or holding them in each hand (so that your body becomes a conductor), or attaching the ends to the two end of a cell battery, to see how the analog value varies depending on voltage.

WARNING! It should go without saying, but I'll say it anyway. When connecting anything electrical up to your micro:bit you should obviously **steer clear of anything involving high voltage mains electricity!**

What Did You Just Learn?

The first thing you learned in this chapter is that I am no electronics engineer. I'm strictly software, you see. But you did go on to learn that even someone as electronically challenged as me can capture some kind of input from a micro:bit pin, and can elicit some kind of output at the self-same pin, both using a few odds and ends I found lying around the house.

If you followed my second to-do suggestion, you also learned about the distinction between binary (on/off) and analog (continuously varying) data.

Research and Resources

While whetting your appetite about programming with pins, in this basic book I have barely scratched the surface. Fortunately, others have scratched way below the surface to produce the plethora of pin programming projects that you will find online. Here is just a small selection to help you take things further:

https://www.microbit.co.uk/musicfest/sequencer

http://make.techwillsaveus.com/projects/micro-graphite-303

http://make.techwillsaveus.com/projects/touch-arpeggiator

http://make.techwillsaveus.com/projects/microguardian

https://microbit0.blob.core.windows.net/pub/xavjevfb/MicroBitBustersIIC2016.pdf

10 – Making Music with the Micro:Bit

While I don't know a lot about electronics (as evidenced in the previous chapter), I do know a little more about music. And so does your micro:bit, which can certainly carry a tune. In this chapter I take you on a brief tour of the micro:bit music making capabilities.

Making Basic Music with the Block Editor

Thanks to the Block Editor's on-screen emulator, we can begin making music with the micro:bit without connecting up a real micro:bit at all *(although I will do so towards the end of the chapter).*

On the left of the following picture you can see the complete set of available **Music** blocks, and on the right of the picture you can see a short tune that I have created by assembling a set of **play tone (Hz)** blocks in sequence.

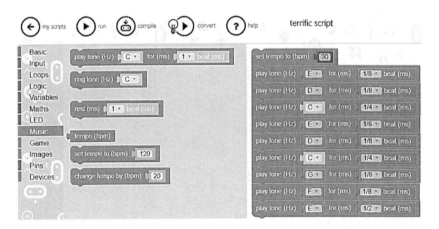

Those blocks play the first nine notes of the tune Three Blind Mice, with the initial **set tempo to (bpm)** block setting the speed of the tune. While this sets the overall speed of the tune, each note has its own relative duration set in "beats".

Playing the Tune

If you press the **compile** button, the code will compile and transfer to your micro:bit which will play the tune (through your attached headphones as described later). Pressing the **run** button should give you a rendition of the tune through your PC speakers... no micro:bit required. It won't sound super, but you should be able to make out the tune.

From Notes to Frequencies

As you can see in my example, for convenience you can specify the names of musical notes in your tunes: **C**, **D**, **E** etc.

It is also possible to specify frequencies in Hz as demonstrated by this script that plays tones of increasing frequency in a `for` loop.

A **for** loop is a loop that runs for a set number of iterations (in this case 101—not 100, because the loop begins at 0) and which sets its index variable (in this case 'i') to the iteration number each time around. Within the loop I am using a multiple of this index value / iteration number to calculate the increasing frequency of the note to play.

Making Music with MicroPython

Now it's time to get a little more serious about making music, by making music with MicroPython. And I take us down this route for two reasons:

- The lack of an on-screen emulator for the MicroPython language means that we must build on the previous pin programming chapter by once again connecting up the micro:bit device to some headphones.
- The music programming possibilities with Python are a little more extensive and (let's be honest) more professional.

Making the Micro:Bit Musical Connection

Connecting up the micro:bit for music is exactly the same as in my simple "click" example of the previous chapter, except that this time we must connect the two wires to **P0** (rather than P2) and **GND** respectively... with the other two ends of those wires connected to the two terminals of a headphone jack. Like this:

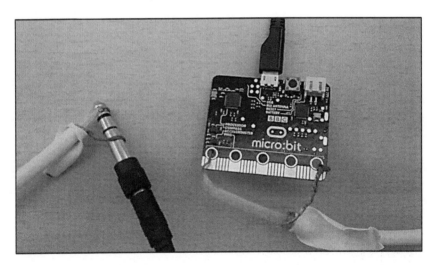

Python Music Programming

When it comes to programming music using Python, it can be as easy as this:

```
1  import music
2
3  tune = ["E:4", "D:4", "C:8","E:4", "D:4","C:8","G:4", "F:3", "F:1","E:8","G
4  music.play(tune)
```

Enter the simple script into the MicroPython Editor, **Download** to your micro:bit, and listen in on your headphones.

The complete code script is:

```
import music

tune = ["E:4", "D:4", "C:8", "E:4", "D:4", "C:8", "G:4",
"F:3", "F:1", "E:8", "G:4", "F:3", "F:1", "E:8"]

music.play(tune)
```

It should be pretty self-explanatory that we `import` the required music library, store a sequence of musical notes as an **array** (list) of **strings** in the `tune` variable, and then `play` the `tune`.

This example takes inspiration from the tune-playing example at microbit-micropython.readthedocs.io/en/latest/tutorials/music.html, but I changed the tune from Frère Jacques to Three Blind Mice. You should see how you too can change the tune if you are musical-minded.

More About MicroPython Music

When making music with MicroPython, you have a few additional options as set out at the aforementioned web address.

You can play prebuilt tunes such as this small selection (of many more):

```
music.play(music.BIRTHDAY)
```

```
music.play(music.WEDDING)
```

```
music.play(music.FUNERAL)
```

And you can program with pitches, as per this simple "siren" example:

```
import music

while True:

    for freq in range(880, 1760, 16):

        music.pitch(freq, 6)

    for freq in range(1760, 880, -16):

        music.pitch(freq, 6)
```

Note that this program runs in a while loop, within which there are two for loops that (respectively) play a series of increasing frequencies followed by a series of decreasing frequencies to sound like a siren. Note the three factors in these for loops that specify the *starting value*, the *end value*, and the *step* (increment amount) to take each time around.

Tony's To-Dos

One thing you might want to do after recreating my Block Editor sample script is convert it to the equivalent Touch Editor code, to see the syntax. And if you're musically-minded, you may well want to create your own musical composition to be compiled to the micro:bit and played to your friends through an attached speaker.

What Did You Just Learn?

In this chapter you learned how to make music with the micro:bit, and even without it. You learned how to play tunes with Python as well as by building tunes in the Block Editor. And in each case, you learned about **for** loops.

Research and Resources

This chapter took you from making music with the Block Editor to making music with MicroPython. When it comes to making music with MicroPython there is no better place to take things further than via the web page at:

microbit-micropython.readthedocs.io/en/latest/tutorials/music.html

That's All, Folks!

Well, that's all folks! The end of this beginners' book of micro:bit basics. I hope you enjoyed it and found it to be a good first step on the road to micro:bit mastery. If you did enjoy it, please take the time to leave a positive review on Amazon.co.uk, Amazon.com or wherever you found it.

Thanks for reading,

Tony

www.microbitbasics.com

Printed in Great Britain
by Amazon